MUCH A JEW ABOUT NOTHING

MUCH A JEW ABOUT NOTHING

A Play

By

Mark Troy

TINSEL ROAD BOOKS

SANTA MONICA, CALIFORNIA

MUCH A JEW ABOUT NOTHING

Copyright © 2010 Mark Troy

Cover art by Ray Cosico

ISBN: 978-0-9819431-7-6

Library of Congress Cataloging-in-Publication-Data is available on file.

Published by Tinsel Road Books
171 Pier Avenue, #328
Santa Monica, California 90405 USA
www.tinselroad.com

americanforests.org
GL**O**BAL
RE**A**LEAF

Tinsel Road Books, in association with Global ReLeaf, will plant two trees for each tree used in the manufacturing of this book. Global ReLeaf is an international campaign by American Forests, the nation's oldest nonprofit conservation organization and a world leader in planting trees for environmental restoration.

Produced by Ronnie Marmo and the 68 Cent Crew Theater Company,
Much a Jew About Nothing originally opened at Theatre 68,
Los Angeles, California on the evening of August 27, 2010.

For my brother Stephen and my sister Renée

(you might not be in show business,
but I love you anyway)

MUCH A JEW ABOUT NOTHING, by Mark Troy was first produced at Theatre 68 in Los Angeles, CA on the 27th of August 2010. Directed by Denny Siegel and produced by Ronnie Marmo with sets designed and constructed by Joe Dallo and lighting and sound designed by Danny Cistone. The stage manager was Connie Avila. The assistant to the playwright was Joanclair Richter.

The cast was as follows:

AFTERPIECE
Setting: Backstage at a Chicago theatre.
LIZZY BERNSTEIN………..…………………......Alice Kalim Lee
PATTY ROZINSK……………………………….Jennifer Sparks

PUPIK
Setting: An apartment in Park Slope, Brooklyn.
HESHE AMSTERDAM………………………….Mitch Lewis
MITZI HOROWITZ…………………..…….Maria Luisa Cianni
JEROME…………………….....…………..…….Goran Ozanic

SISTER SNELL
Setting: Chicago architectural firm.
BERNICE SNELL...………..…………....……………Katy Jacoby
MARY……………………..…...…………..……...Connie Avila
CHARLOTTE BURDICK………………....AnneMaria Mignini

THE MODERN AMERICAN ROMANCE NOT OFTEN SEEN
Setting: Small apartment. Anywhere, USA.
DEEDEE FISHMAN…………………....…..…………..Melanie Blue
AVERY MINOWITZ………………………………Joe Massingill

HOOD RATZ
Setting: Fairfax district of Los Angeles.
BEN KATZ…...…………………..…………….Bryan Deehring
ARTHUR KATZ…………..…...…....…………….....Chad Addison
SALLY PEABODY……………………………..Claudine Claudio
                                    (*Understudy: Denny Siegel)
YEWANDE MANATOBA……………..…………..Leo J. Clark

AFTERPIECE

Backstage of Chicago's Dramatists Center. Big stage, big audience, loads of applause as LIZZY BERNSTEIN, wearing a ton too much makeup and a stage costume that is both poorly made and overdone, enters. SHE is playing a socialite, with jewels, heels, and a hat that doesn't seem to fit well. Behind HER is PATTY ROZINSKY, in a bikini -- seems they couldn't possibly be in the same play.

LIZZY immediately sits and removes her makeup. PATTY reaches for a robe and a cigarette.

LIZZY. I get the short Jewish guy in the front row with the blue tie.

PATTY. You saw me point to him. Didn't you see me point to the short Jewish guy in the front row with the blue tie?

LIZZY. When did you point to the short Jewish guy in the front row with the blue tie?

PATTY. You saw me point to him.

LIZZY. There was no signal.

PATTY. It was a signal. As clear as day a signal.

LIZZY. You're wrong. Let's just drop it. (*Beat*) You went up on your line tonight.

PATTY. What line did I go up on tonight?

LIZZY. You know the line.

PATTY. If I knew the line...

LIZZY. Act one, scene four.

PATTY. Act one, scene four... I'm not in act one, scene four.

LIZZY. You're not? This play is very confusing.

Reaches over for a puff of PATTY's cigarette.

PATTY. *(Mumbles)* I gave you the signal. *(Louder)* -- I gave you the signal, Lizzy -- that the short Jewish guy in the front row with the blue tie was all mine. I remember distinctly. I went like this... *(Twitches her ear and points)* ...in act two, scene three.

LIZZY. I'm already dead in act two, scene three.

PATTY. You die in this play?

LIZZY. Oh no. Did I come out on stage in act two, scene three?

PATTY. Yes. Yes I think you did come out on stage in act two, scene three. You did come out. I handed you the phone when it rang.

LIZZY. I was going to ask you about that. Doesn't this play take place in the early sixteen hundreds? Cuz there would be no phone.

PATTY. We should e-mail the writer and ask.

LIZZY. I had to ad lib. Into the phone. I said something about my character being late for an appointment, or something, with her daughter.

PATTY. Except she has no children because of the farming accident.

LIZZY. Which I forgot because there wasn't supposed to be a phone. I'm gonna get a note on that from the director.

PATTY. How long have we been performing this piece a crap?

LIZZY. I lost count somewhere in Baltimore.

PATTY. I still don't understand... completely... what is that word -- the plot?

LIZZY. Oh, Patty, that's the easy part of this production. You see, you're playing the young ingenue who... who... *(Looks at HER bikini)* Is that your costume every night?

PATTY. In the second act. In the first act I'm in a space suit.

LIZZY. What am I in, in the first act?

PATTY. I'm really not sure. Do we have a scene together?

LIZZY. I have a better question. What happened to that Catholic tall guy, center section, three from the end that was at the matinee this afternoon?

PATTY. I invited him back here.

LIZZY. You invited the Catholic tall guy, center section, three from the end that was at the matinee -- back here? He was mine! I invited him back here!

PATTY. I gave you the signal! *(Does the signal again)* Like this... right at the top of act one, scene two -- before the dinner scene.

LIZZY. You did that signal for the Catholic tall guy, center section, three from the end that was at the matinee to meet you back here at the top of act one, scene two before the dinner scene?

PATTY. Yes.

LIZZY. But act one, scene two is my attempted suicide scene. I could never see the signal what with my head that deep in the toilet bowl trying to drown myself because I don't have a daughter.

PATTY. *(Long beat.)* You have a suicide scene?

LIZZY. I don't? Now I'm going to get a note on that from the director.

LIZZY pulls the ugly dress off over HER head to reveal another ugly dress underneath. SHE stares at it.

LIZZY. Please dear god tell me I made the costume change at the end of act three, scene one.

PATTY. I don't think you did tonight, Lizzy.

LIZZY. I played the entire third act as the woman who got murdered in the second act?

PATTY. They probably won't notice. It's a very convoluted play. And we're not very good in it.

LIZZY. You're being kind, Patty. Not only are we not very good in it, we're downright pitiful. I mean, we stink. We're not actors. I don't know how we got these jobs.

PATTY. I slept with the producer.

LIZZY. Oh so did I, you think that had something to do with it?

PATTY. *(Shrugs, then cuts her toenails)* At least the audiences are still coming after fifteen cities...

LIZZY. We must have a buzz.

PATTY. We must. Tonight, half the audience was filled with men from the mental facility at Chicago General.

LIZZY. You mean the short Jewish guy in the front row with the blue tie has a mental illness?

PATTY. Lizzy. Have you called Jack?

LIZZY. You know I did. You call Jake?

PATTY. *(Nods)* Jack and Jake were called.

LIZZY. Which leaves us in a strange city, in a horrible play, doing bad acting, trying to pick up men who dribble for a living.

PATTY. You ever feel bad, Lizzy?

LIZZY. About not being a very good actress? Does Meryl Streep?

PATTY. Oh she sucks!

THEY burst out laughing.

LIZZY. Or or... Shirley MacLaine?

PATTY. What about... about... Dame Judy Dench?

LIZZY. *(Takes a soda and blows it out HER nose)* They think they put a "Dame" in front of their names -- suddenly they have talent. Excuse me, from now on call me Dame Lizzy Bernstein.

PATTY. Dame Patty Rozinsky at your service for drama, comedy, farce, thriller or, if I am lucky... exploitation.

The laughter is boisterous.

PATTY . *(Short beat as she takes the soda from LIZZY and drinks)* When I asked if you ever felt bad... it wasn't acting I was asking about.

LIZZY. *(Hurt)* I know.

LIZZY pulls the dress SHE has on over HER head to reveal the exact same bikini PATTY has on.

THEY look at each for a beat, shocked.

LIZZY. Oh shit.

PATTY. Are you playing the part of Alice, the sharp witted, yet naive young school girl that is taken in by the acerbic matriarch of a Connecticut family only to find they're cannibals and when the mother commits suicide, you marry her husband, eat her, and steal all the money to build the world's largest swimming pool -- or am I?

LIZZY. *(Looks at HER outfit)* I guess I should be.

PATTY goes to LIZZY and takes the hat. Puts it on. It fits perfectly.

PATTY. We're definitely going to get notes on that from the director.

LIZZY. What have we been doing? We've really been screwing up!

PATTY. I'll tell you what we've been doing, Lizzy. And it's not something Jack or Jake better ever find out about.

LIZZY. We've cheated on our husbands.

PATTY. Four months on the road... eight shows a week... that's a lot a cheating.

LIZZY. Have you spoken to anyone else in the cast? Asked them what they've been doing after shows. Maybe we're not the only ones missing our spouses, and humping every Tom, Dick, or mental patient we can see through the foot-lights. You should ask someone.

PATTY. I can't ask anyone, Lizzy.

LIZZY. Why not?

PATTY. We're in a two character play. We play all the parts.

LIZZY. We're the entire cast? *(PATTY nods)* That means we're the only ones who are screwing around while our husbands wait back home... thinking we're big stars in a big show? *(PATTY nods)* I didn't know the theater was full of all this... weakness of the flesh. Cheating. Falling in love. Copping a feel with a stage-hand.

PATTY. Hey. I gave you a signal about that stage-hand.

LIZZY. This is our life now. In spite of the fact that we think we suck at this, the audiences, the reviews... people think we have talent.
PATTY. You're right, Lizzy... we gotta hold this together. We weren't looking for this. This was just supposed to be a fun summer for us.

LIZZY. Summer stock is going to kill our marriages!

PATTY. Everyone in show business knows what goes on.

LIZZY. Even Meryl Streep?

PATTY. Oh she's so awful -- who would "do her?"

LIZZY. Alright... we need a diversion.

PATTY. From our diversions?

LIZZY. Let's concentrate on the work.

PATTY. This lousy play?

LIZZY. Yes. Concentrate on it. Put all we have into it. Stop picking out cute guys in the audience. Study our lines. Learn the play. Please, Patty... I don't want to lose Jack.

PATTY. No more goofing off? Yes. We pledge to the drama of our show.

THEY put their hands over their hearts.

PATTY/LIZZY. When in the course of human events an actress steps on stage - she shall not step into another actor's sight line, steal focus or mug to the audience, touch her hair, forget her lines, miss her entrances, drop cues, or cop a feel from a stage hand.

LIZZY. I need a drink.

PATTY nods as intermission BELL rings.

PATTY. Fuck... is there an Act six is this stinker?

LIZZY. Who am I playing?

PATTY. How the hell should I know? I don't even know who I'm playing.

LIZZY. Doesn't this play ever end!?!

THEY grab as many of the costumes as THEY can, and exit.

LIGHTS.

PUPIK

A small, lonely-looking one-bedroom apartment on the 56th block in Brooklyn, New York. A worn sofa, end table, rocking chair, and 19 inch black and white TV.

HESHE AMSTERDAM, 70s, shuffles into the room with a tray of cheese and crackers. HE looks around for a spot to place the dish. HE tries a few. Finally, HE just eats the cheese while standing. Finished, HE exits and returns with two glasses of Manischewitz. HE tries a few places to put the glasses but is unsatisfied and drinks both. Exit to the kitchen. On the third run, HE comes in with a bowl of soup. Doesn't even look for a place, stands and slurps it up. The doorbell rings. It's to the tune of <u>Hava Nagila</u>.

HE runs the soup back into the kitchen and comes back in fluffing each pillow on HIS way to the door.

HESHE. *(Joyously)* Pupik! My *pupik!* Where is my *pupik?*

HE opens door and enter MITZI HOROWITZ, 20s, beautifully dressed with a big smile, and a giant hug for HIM.

MITZI. Uncle Heshe!

HESHE. My sweet *Pupik.*

MITZI. Oh, Uncle Heshe... it's been too long.

HESHE. No. I raced to the door as soon as you rang. Come in, come in, my sweet *pupik.*

MITZI. You have been calling me that name since I was five years old. My dear Uncle Heshe.

HESHE. That's because you always had the sweetest *pupik*. *(Grabs HER around the waist and plays with her belly button)* There it is. There it is. What a *pupik*!

MITZI. Ticklish! Ticklish!

HESHE. I've tickled a lot of *pupik's* in my day. Yours is -- perfection.

MITZI. Let me see how good you look, Uncle Heshe.

HESHE. I don't like to say it, but I look good.

MITZI. Your skin is glowing.

HESHE. I don't like to say it, but my skin glows.

MITZI. And you're getting exercise? How many miles a day are you walking?

HESHE. On the treadmill, one hour a day. With it turned on -- <u>half</u> an hour. Just over a mile and a little short of a stroke.

MITZI. Even your teeth look extra white, Uncle Heshe.

HESHE. I don't like to say it, but these teeth cost me a fortune. And they come out at night! *(THEY laugh and hug again)* It's so wonderful to see you. Mitzi. Let me look at <u>you</u>. Geez, you're a woman now.

MITZI. I'm thirty-five.

HESHE. A real woman. With a very nice *tuchas*.

MITZI. You were never one to hold back what you were thinking, Uncle Heshe. No matter how outrageous or inappropriate.

HESHE. That's because I believe in the human condition. That as a species we need to evolve and be free of any political correctness. To say what we mean, and to mean what we say. When I say you have a nice *tuchas*, it is not for any sexual overtones, it is merely an observation. And a fact.

MITZI. And that is why you are my favorite uncle.

HESHE. Why don't I get you some cheese and crackers, Mitzi?

MITZI. I would love some cheese and crackers.

HESHE. I ate all the cheese and crackers. See. I am evolving as a species. I am telling the truth. Do you watch the news these days? They're not telling the truth. It's all a spin machine. This person believes in something and then makes the argument to fit *that* something. It's not the truth. It's *their* truth. How about some good Kosher Manischewitz wine?

MITZI. I would love some good Kosher Manischewitz wine.

HESHE. I've already put it away, plus I'm too tired to pull it out. You see I asked you, but I also told you the reality of the situation. Do you listen to talk radio these days? They have a one track mind. I'm not sure if an original thought hit them, they would know what to do with it. I know what to do with original thought, Mitzi. I have original thought. I speak what is on my mind. Kippered herring?

MITZI. You don't have any kippered herring, do you?

HESHE. Not anymore. So tell me about you-know-who. What's his name?

MITZI. *(Beaming)* Jerome.

HESHE. Jerome? Jerome is a good name for a future husband.

MITZI. It is, isn't it.

HESHE. I don't like the names they're calling their kids today. Gaga. Diddy. 50 Cents? What kind of name is this? That's not a name -- it's a currency.

MITZI. I am so glad you are in good spirits, Uncle Heshe.

HESHE. My ticker's still ticking, and my shitter's still shitting. How can I complain?

MITZI. And emotionally...?

HESHE. We don't look back at the past, Mitzi. Do you read magazines these days? They dwell on everything old. They never see the future as anything that might be good. They only tell us how things were better in the old days. Let me tell them something, Mitzi -- tomorrow -- today is the old days. A toast to you and Jerome. A strong Jewish name. He is strong and Jewish right?

MITZI. Huh? Oh yeah. Very, very... Jewish. And strong.

HESHE. And he has good character?

MITZI. He does.

HESHE. What about the ankles?

MITZI. Hmm?

HESHE. A man should have strong ankles. It shows he will work hard and can carry the load of family and wife.

MITZI. I'll have to look next time.

HESHE. Do that and get back to me.

MITZI. Uncle Heshe, you were the first person I thought of when I accepted Jerome's hand in marriage. I had to come see you.

HESHE. Oh. I've been cooking. I know how you like to eat. I wanted to make your favorites. I got the recipe off the computer.

MITZI. You do internet?

HESHE. No. My cooking book was sitting on the computer. I know nothing about computers. *(HE reaches for the book)* I'm not even sure why your cousin Ralphie bought it for me.

MITZI. I'm sure he just wanted you to have the experience of the World Wide Web.

HESHE. Did you know your cousin Alison did a spread in Maxim Magazine.

MITZI. I saw it, she looked beautiful.

HESHE. Porno.

MITZI. No, Uncle Heshe, it's a classy magazine.

HESHE. I didn't look at it. *(Opens book)* I made you... Sephardic Dandelion soup with chick-peas, ground cumin, spinach, and beef tri-tips.

MITZI. Uncle Heshe, I don't eat meat.

HESHE. We're eating out. I'm taking you both out. You name the place.

MITZI. You didn't have to go through all this trouble for us.

HESHE. Trouble? This is an important day in your life. <u>The</u> most important day of your life. And I don't like to say it, but you're my favorite niece. And that includes nephews. And my own children. So where is he?

MITZI. He's parking the car. He'll be here any minute. Uncle Heshe, I wonder if we could talk about --

HESHE. -- I've asked you, Mitzi, not to bring it up. *(Long Pause)* If there is one thing I cannot bring up is even her name. Not even her name.

MITZI. Sometimes talking about a loss helps --

HESHE. -- Married forty-seven years! Did you know we were married forty-seven years?

MITZI. Yes, Uncle Heshe.

HESHE. Forty-seven years. And the time she was ill... do not talk about the years of her illness, Mitzi.

MITZI. I promise, Uncle Heshe.

HESHE. Five years since she left us, and I have never uttered nor heard her name in this house. I couldn't handle it. It would destroy me all over again. It just plain hurts. You don't spend that much time with somebody and then one day they're not there, and poof, you get over it.

MITZI. Have you been sleeping?

HESHE. It's cold.

MITZI. And her stuff...?

HESHE. I've tried putting it in bags to send to Goodwill, but when I hold it in my hands, I can't get the strength to put it in the bag.

MITZI. I understand.

HESHE. You're starting your life, Mitzi. A whole new life. This brings such joy to me. I'm a *Der zokn* - an old man, and I can finally see some good, some happiness in someone's future. *Mazel Tov* to you and Jerome. And I wish on you as much years of happiness and *nachas* that that woman gave to me in a lifetime.

MITZI. *(Consoling HIM)* I want you to love Jerome as much as I do.

HESHE. If you love him, then I love him. I consider him my own son. My own child. I will do for him the *Mezinka*. A special dance for parents whose last child is getting married. You're like my child, Mitzi. Here's my dance.

HE does a wonderful dance which makes HER smile. Then there is a soft knock at the door.

HESHE . Go, go. The boy should see my Mezinka with his own eyes.

MITZI opens the door and JEROME enters. HE is dressed like Moses: Long white undertunic, blue vest, sandals, carrying a staff. HESHE practically falls off HIS feet at the sight. THEY stare for a beat, each unwilling to break the silence.

HESHE. So. Mitzi tells me you're Jewish.

MITZI. Uncle Heshe. This is Jerome. Jerome, my favorite Uncle Heshe.

HESHE. Uh-huh. Perhaps I <u>will</u> bust out that Manischewitz. Excuse me. *(Mumbles to HIMself)* I was going to give that *putz* a *mezinka*.

HE exits. JEROME falls apart.

JEROME. Oh my god -- he hates me.

MITZI. He's just in shock.

JEROME. I told you this wouldn't work.

MITZI. What's not working?

JEROME. I look like I'm going to a toga party.

MITZI. You look cute.

JEROME. Yes. If this was 1200 B.C.

MITZI. Calm down, Jerome.

JEROME. Your uncle is never going to fall for this. It's not like I'm not Jewish.

MITZI. You are Jewish. You are Jewish, Jerome. Just not the kind of Jewish my parents like.

JEROME. This is crazy!

MITZI. My uncle Heshe is Orthodoxy. They don't play games. They're the modern classification for the traditional section of Jewry that upholds the *halakhic* way of life as illustrated in a divinely ordained Torah.

JEROME. What do you think <u>we</u> read in temple -- Oprah Magazine?

MITZI. I'm serious, Jerome. Uncle Heshe can make things much easier for us when you meet my parents.

JEROME. You've told me this a thousand times, it doesn't make sense.

MITZI. You're a Reconstructionist, Jerome. You might as well be Lutheran.

JEROME. Hey, my family is as Jewish as the next Jew. We overflow with Jew. We're bursting with Jew. We're the Everlasting *Gobstoppers* of *Jewdom!*

MITZI. I'm telling you, my father would have you shot. He respects his brother Heshe. He'll listen to him. If Uncle Heshe likes you, then he can convince my parents that you're acceptable. And we can get married.

JEROME. Why is this so complicated?

MITZI. You grew up Reformed, Jerome. Your mission is "to create and sustain vibrant Jewish congregations wherever Reform Jews live." La la la. <u>Our</u> mission is to make you guys look Catholic.

JEROME. Hey. A million and a half Jews consider themselves Reformed.

MITZI. How can so many be so wrong?

JEROME. Why can't we just love each other and stand apart from your parents?

MITZI. My father is worth twelve million dollars and I'm an only child.

JEROME. Do you think I look more Jewish <u>with</u> the staff or without?

MITZI. I can't believe I fell in love with someone outside my faith.

JEROME. Hey, hey. You're just more religious is all. We're not a lower class of people than you.

MITZI. To some.

JEROME. What?

MITZI. Well, we only formally disagree about every issue including the level of observance.

JEROME. And don't forget our histrionic long-standing disagreement on how many presents to give out on Hanukkah -- one for the whole holiday or eight - one for each night.

MITZI. Very funny. You get ONE present, Jerome.

JEROME. *(Rolls HIS eyes)* Eight! You get eight!

MITZI. Shhh. Uncle Heshe will hear you!

JEROME. Hey, we're all gettin' into Heaven, baby -- the Chosen People.

MITZI. We'll see.

HE double-takes.

JEROME. You're taking this much too seriously, Honey. Your parents can't be tricked. And don't you think Uncle Heshe will see through this? I am coming on a little strong in this get-up.

MITZI. Heshe's worth ten million dollars and he hates his own kids.

JEROME. Does this tunic make me look fat?

HESHE enters with three glasses and the bottle of wine.

HESHE. There's only a little left because I drank most of it just now. Sit down. Let's get to know each other. Pull up a rock or something...*(Laughs)* A chair. I made a little funny. Like I was thinking in there... if for lunch we could go someplace where Jerome can slaughter a calf in front of us -- that could be nice. *(More laughs)* Tell him, Mitzi. Tell him about your Uncle Heshe.

MITZI. Uncle Heshe believes in the human condition. That as a species we need to evolve and be free of any political correctness. To say what we mean --

HESHE/MITZI. -- and to mean what we say.

HESHE. *(Raises HIS glass)* I say Jerome... you're a fake.

JEROME panics and look at MITZI.

HESHE A fraud. *La'chaim.* Drink, drink.

MITZI. Uncle Heshe... please let me explain...

HESHE. What makes you think this needs an explanation? You call me, you tell me you met the man of your dreams, and say I should meet him. Even before your own parents. I invite you over for meat, and Moses walks through the door. And he's mute.

MITZI. Say something. Anything. Jerome.

JEROME. *(Stammers)* I was very unhappy to hear about the loss of your wife.

HESHE. *(Stiffening)* What?

MITZI. *(Sotto)* Oh no.

JEROME. You lost your wife of forty-seven years.

HESHE. Why are you bringing this up?

JEROME. She's dead, right?

MITZI. Jerome!

HESHE. You bring this up in my house? You come into my home and bring this up?

JEROME. These things happen. It helps to talk about it. I lost a cat once and couldn't eat for a week!

HESHE. You mention this in my home? In front of my ears? *Oye gevalt!*

MITZI. Uncle Heshe! Jerome --

JEROME. Please, Mitzi. I know what I'm doing. She was obviously old, what was her name... Ida?

HESHE. Her name! HER NAME! IN MY HOUSE!

MITZI. Let's all calm down. Have something to nosh. I'll eat meat, it'll be fun.

JEROME. Ida is a pretty name. My cat's name was Bertha. Where is she buried? The wife, not the cat.

HESHE. I'm having a heart attack.

JEROME. Or was she cremated? People do that now. With Bertha --

MITZI. -- Jerome, stop it.

JEROME. What? *(Whispers)* I want him to like me.

HESHE. *(Races around the room)* Where's my *siddur*... my *siddur*, where is it? This is a catastrophe. A *shonda* it is! He mentioned my dear Ida.

MITZI. Uncle Heshe - you said her name.

HESHE. I did. *(Prays)* Yit'gadal v'yit'kadash sh'mei raba...

MITZI. Amen.

JEROME. *(A beat late)* Amen.

HESHE. B'al'ma di v'ra khir'utei...

MITZI. Amen...

JEROME. *(Half a beat off)* Amen. *(Falters) V'yam'likh mal'khutei b--'dhay--*

HESHE. *V'yam'likh mal'khutei b'chayeikhon uv'yomeikhon...*

HESHE stops and lets JEROME continue alone...
JEROME . *"...Da doo ron ron ron da doo ron ron. He looked so quiet, but my oh my -- Da doo ron ron ron da doo ron ron." (Stops, embarrassed)* Ron.

HESHE. *(Long pause)* Give me those ankles!

JEROME. What?

MITZI. Uncle Heshe...

HESHE. Give me those god-damn ankles... I want to see those ankles!!

HESHE chases JEROME around the room trying to grab HIS feet...

JEROME. Is this some sort of fetish...?

HESHE. Get over here, chicken. I want those ankles. That's all the proof I need. Then I'm calling my brother and his wife and we're sending Mitzi to live on a *kibbutz.*

HESHE finally gets JEROME on the sofa, pulls at HIS feet, yanks down HIS socks and grabs HIS ankles.

HESHE . AHA! I knew it! Weak ankles!

MITZI. Uncle Heshe...

HESHE. No, no. These are not strong ankles. It shows he will not work hard and cannot carry the load of family and wife.

JEROME. Ticklish! Ticklish!

HESHE pushes JEROME's leg away.

HESHE. This man is an imposter.

MITZI. No. Uncle Heshe... please let me explain...

HESHE. How can you explain?

MITZI. I can't explain.

JEROME. I can explain. I'm Jewish. Tell him, Mitzi, I'm Jewish all over. I can do a prayer. *(Reads without any problem)* Barukh ata Adonai Eloheinu Melekh haolam, bo're p'ri ha'adama.

MITZI. Good boy, Jerome.

HESHE. Perfect. He just gave us the prayer for the eating of non-fruit produce. Like <u>that</u> comes in handy a lot!

MITZI. Still. It was a nice job.

HESHE. I knew it. I might be old, but I wouldn't fall for this... this... this costume!

JEROME. I happen to be a professional actor.

HESHE. *Oye. Gevalt.*

JEROME. Uh-huh. Currently I am in a small but completely well-received production of "Jesus Christ Superstar"--

MITZI. *Oye. Gevalt.*

JEROME. -- at the thirty-two seat Washington Square Theater Complex, and I happen to have this costume... *(To MITZI without a breath)* ... he shouldn't know I'm playing Jesus Christ, right, that would not be a good thing for him to know or to tell your father, right?

HESHE. The boy plays Jesus Christ. *(Beat)* Jesus Christ!

MITZI. It's just his job, Uncle Heshe.

HESHE. I know. But that's just what Jesus Christ said! *(Like Jesus)* It's just my job... come on Mary Magdalen, we're going to supper. Sure, invite our friend Judas Iscariot. Invite all the boys. We'll take a picture. Then I'll take the hit for all the shenanigans that's been going on, and *oye gevalt* --they'll crucify me... <u>it's my job!</u>

HESHE pours the wine and drinks.

HESHE. My wife... my dear Ida... If she were alive today to see her favorite niece marry you... it would destroy her. *(Harshly to HER)* How I can explain this to your parents? To your father! Jerome is not Jewish!

MITZI. He is, he is, Uncle Heshe.

HESHE. Don't tell me he is. We'd be better off if he was Black. Then we explain "these things happen" but how can we explain a weak-ankled non-believer like Jerome as your fiancé?

JEROME. I believe. I had a *Bar Mitzvah.* And a *Bris.* Here, look --

HE starts to pull up the tunic but Mitzi slaps HIS hand down.

HESHE. Reformed *Bar Mitzvah?*

JEROME. I read from the Torah. I did my *hof'torah*... Phonetically. Then we had a party. We danced to Engelbert Humperdinck. My grandmother threw out her hip.

MITZI. I don't think you're helping, Jerome.

JEROME. No. I'm going to stand up for my people.

HESHE. <u>Your</u> people? You don't have people. You took what you liked from my people and disregarded anything that wasn't easy and you called it <u>your</u> people.

MITZI. He's got a point.

HESHE. There's no work on the Sabbath, but you decide, shopping at Target is more important than God, so you shop. There's no eating cheese and meat together. But you like McDonald's, so there goes god's other law. You don't fast when you're supposed to, you don't pray when you're supposed to, you don't go to *shul* when you're supposed to... because it's just not convenient. And you call that Religion.

MITZI. Uncle Heshe...

HESHE. Don't slow me down Mitzi, I'm on a roll.

JEROME. I don't call that religion, Uncle Heshe, I call that honor. Truthfulness to myself and to my soul.

MITZI. No, Jerome.

HESHE. Let the heathen talk. I'll pour more wine. *(HE does so)*

JEROME. I'm just like you in many ways, Heshe. I don't speak in political correctness. I don't pretend to carry the party line and I don't pretend I'm someone I'm not. *(THEY stare at HIS get-up)* Usually. That's right. I have just as much rights to carry on the Jewish faith as you do.

HESHE. Do you know who you're talking to? I was a cantor at my temple for nineteen years before I couldn't hit the high notes anymore. I raised thousands of dollars for Russian Jewry and to plant trees in Tel Aviv. I have been to the Wailing Wall six times. I climbed Mount Sinai. And more importantly... I studied Torah. Sacred Jewish writings: eternally valid moral principles. My life is settled upon both the Written Law, the first five books of the Old Testament, and the

Oral Law of the codified in the Mishna and interpreted in the Talmud. I keep Kosher and observe all the traditions of the Jewish faith even though I am completely baffled by many of them. What have <u>you</u> done?

JEROME. I've spoken to god.

HESHE. *Oysgehorevet. (To MITZI)* He talks to god.

JEROME. In my own way. In my own way I have heard his word. And that word is just as valid as your word.

HESHE. Anyone can make up their own religions these days. Just like Bill O'Reilly. Their own rules. It's not proper. Making up your own rules.

JEROME. I have rules. My rules. The rules of love and unconditional acceptance. The rules of heart, and passion. I love Mitzi, not because she's a certain kind of Jewish person, but because her heart is pure. As is mine.

HESHE. Did God tell you that in one of your late night on-line chats?

JEROME. Do you watch the news these days? They're not telling the truth. It's all a spin machine. This person believes in something and then makes the argument to fit *that* something. It's like religion. Do we believe a god created the Earth in seven days, or do we believe in evolution. Or can we believe in both? It's just an argument... an ever changing, evolving, argument. It will go on forever. But I would think God did this on purpose. After all, if god is smart enough to create all of this, why did he bother to give us free will to counter and question his every divine move?

HESHE. You watch the spin machines?

JEROME. I do.

MITZI. You're both alike, Uncle Heshe. Stubborn in your ways. Defiant in your individual beliefs. You and Jerome are like the same person. There isn't a drop of political correctness in either of you.

JEROME. I'm sorry I said anything to hurt you, Uncle Heshe.

HESHE. I suppose we do share some... similarities.

JEROME. Of course we do. We both know it doesn't matter what you call yourself, it's who you are.

HESHE. You know, I think I like him better than my own Alison, the Queen of Maxim Magazine. Who one day *goyim will* be going through a curtain at the back of a video store to see her movies.

JEROME. There's something else God told me, Uncle Heshe. You're not Jewish either.

HESHE. Oh?

JEROME. Not about costumes, or ankles, or... love. You're not Jewish either.

HESHE. Why you little --

JEROME. It's very clear in all the texts. The real Jewish man, woman or child, must go to the Promised Land and live there and defend it.

HESHE. Are you crazy?! They got guns there.

JEROME. Then you also are playing a little game of words. Of convenience. Of easiness.

HESHE. *(Long beat)* Moses is right. A real Jew doesn't live in Park Slope. He lives in the Holy Land. I know that. Your father knows that.

MITZI. Then you will tell mom and dad that you've given Jerome and I your blessings of marriage?

HESHE. My little *pupik* girl is going to marry Jerome and make lots of little Conservative Jews together.

JEROME. Reformed.

MITZI. Orthodox.

HESHE. *(Wipes eyes with hanky)* Love can be such a beautiful thing. I had forgotten.

MITZI. Uncle Heshe... you're thinking of Aunt Ida.

JEROME. Your dead wife.

MITZI throws HIM a look. HESHE nods.

HESHE. Let's go. I'm taking you to eat. A nice Kosher vegetarian restaurant. If such a thing exists. And then I'm going to first pack your Aunt Ida's clothes and take them all to Good Will.

MITZI. Oh, Uncle Heshe. That's wonderful.

HESHE. Then I'm going to Israel.

MITZI. That's extreme.

HESHE. Come! We dance. The *Mezinka*. It's tradition...

HESHE starts to dance as HESHE and MITZI clap. HE is euphoric.

JEROME. Can I join in?

HESHE. Not with those ankles.

MITZI pulls JEROME back from dancing as the lights slowly fade.

SISTER SNELL

The offices of Poxner and Poser Architects, in Venice, California. Mahogany desk, center, door; at right. BERNICE SNELL, 30s, enters. SHE is in a full nuns outfit with habit, guimpe, and coif. SHE rants to no one in particular.

BERNICE. Jesus Christ! God-damn it -- who do I have to fuck around here to get anything done!? *Again.* St. Fabiola is never going to find the recognition it deserves if this work does not get done. This work <u>must</u> get done! Hello? *(Into intercom on the desk)* Mary, Jesus and Joseph! Are you out there? Oh shit... Mary? Are you out there?!?

MARY (OFF-STAGE). *(Calmly)* Yes, Ms. Snell.

BERNICE. Don't give me any attitude, Mary -- what the hell is going on? Has the shipment of stained glass arrived at the construction site?

MARY (OFF-STAGE). Yes, Ms. Snell.

BERNICE. And there was no problem with the inventory?

MARY (OFF-STAGE). No, Ms. Snell.

BERNICE. Good. My skin crawls when there's problems.

MARY (OFF-STAGE). There was this one problem, Ms. Snell.

BERNICE. Jesus H. -- what's the problem?

MARY (OFF-STAGE). The stained glass you ordered for St. Fabiola is... is...

BERNICE. Well what the F-- is it, Mary?

MARY (OFF-STAGE). It's Jewish, Ms. Snell.

BERNICE. I ordered *Jewish* stained glass for St. Fabiola? Who am I --
the devil?! A dybbuk? *(Sits, lights a cigarette)* What am I supposed to do
with Jewish stained-glass?

MARY (OFF-STAGE). Yeah that is a problem. Of course not as big
a problem as the fact that they have Jewish stars all over them. And a
likenesses of Moses. And King David. And a *dreidel.*

BERNICE. Would you shut up already. Shit. Where are my pills?
(Searching drawers) Where is god's name is the Zoloft? Mary? Are you
out there?

MARY (OFF-STAGE). *(Even more calmly)* Ms. Snell, the doctor
refused to extend your prescription for the Zoloft.

BERNICE. Why would that A-hole do that?

MARY (OFF-STAGE). He'd never heard of anyone being on Zoloft
since fourth grade.

BERNICE. Uh-huh, uh-huh, well what the hell does he know -- the
man hangs around sick people all day. He has no idea the pressures
I'm under.

MARY (OFF-STAGE). You *were* married to him, Ms. Snell.
BERNICE. Uh-huh, uh-huh. Only briefly. I spent more time married
to the pharmacist. At least with him, I knew I would come home to a
nice meal and a big bowl of Zoloft! Okay... get on the horn and get
that distributor to take back those dreidels.

MARY (OFF-STAGE). What excuse shall I use, Ms. Snell?

BERNICE. Start with... the good patrons of Chicago's newest and
most brilliant designed downtown church, St. Fabiola, sees no need

in bringing Jews into the congregation. Blah blah blah, and sign your own name. I don't want my name on such a blasphemous letter. I think I'm having an attack...

MARY (OFF-STAGE). You're not smoking in there, are you, Ms. Snell?

BERNICE. Don't be a stupid monkey, Mary. It's just my usual panic.

MARY (OFF-STAGE). Because if you started smoking again, you made me promise I would tell your psychiatrist.

BERNICE. Uh-huh uh-huh... Well he can go straight to hell.

MARY (OFF-STAGE). He cares about you.

BERNICE. Marry a man for six months, he wants to run your life. I'm not smoking! *(Puts out cigarette)* Mary. Has the giant two story cross arrived at the warehouse yet?

MARY (OFF-STAGE). Yes, Ms. Snell.

BERNICE. Good, good. At least we are on schedule with that! That cross is the cornerstone of St. Fabiola and brings with it the religious strength and virtuosity blah blah blah that is going to take me to the pinnacle of my career and put me in the history books of great architects.

MARY (OFF-STAGE). It's got an extra plank of wood attached to it.

BERNICE. Holy crap!

MARY (OFF-STAGE). They tell me that instead of the standard... one up and one across plank, this one has one up, one across and another one up. It looks like the number "four."

BERNICE. I'm fucked.

MARY (OFF-STAGE). *(Knowing the truth)* So that's not how you designed it, Ms. Snell?

BERNICE. Where's my *Ritalin*?

MARY (OFF-STAGE). Uh-huh uh-huh -- all out.

BERNICE. How can a person be paranoid in this office without their drugs! Christ Almighty -- this whole project is shooting down the toilet. Mary - where's Joseph? I need Joseph. What's Joseph doing?

MARY (OFF-STAGE). He's working on the plans for the rec center, Ms. Snell.

BERNICE. And Jesus?

MARY (OFF-STAGE). *Haysuse?*

BERNICE. Get his butt in here. This place is falling apart. And my asthma is a real bastard today.
MARY (OFF-STAGE). Yes, Ms. Snell.

BERNICE. You're a crack-head, Mary, you know that?

MARY (OFF-STAGE). I do the best with what I've got, Ms. Snell.

BERNICE. Everybody who has ever worked for me has disappointed me. Is my appointment here yet?

MARY (OFF-STAGE). She's in the ladies room. Throwing up.

BERNICE. About seeing me? I'm a pussy cat.

MARY (OFF-STAGE). You're an evil C-word, Ms. Snell, that's your reputation.

BERNICE. Who in fuck's sake is saying that?

MARY (OFF-STAGE). Who isn't?

BERNICE. I have an exemplary reputation. I'll freakin' break the bloody neck of anyone who says otherwise. Now you march yourself into that bathroom and stop that woman from vomiting in my building.

MARY (OFF-STAGE). Yes, Ms. Snell.

SHE reaches for a cigarette, then changes HER mind.

BERNICE. Six months. Six months I've been trying to find someone to paint that god forsaken mural in the new church vestibule. The entire project depends on it. Damn it, all I get are *taggers* and leftists who have no idea what this magnificent church blah blah blah -- is going to do to my career!

SHE squats to pick up a pencil on the floor as... CHARLOTTE BURDICK enters. In a business suit, carrying giant portfolio too large for HER to maneuver. SHE sees BERNICE on the ground looking like SHE's praying. BERNICE turns.

BERNICE. Yeah. What the balls are you staring at?

CHARLOTTE. I thought... I thought you were... praying.

BERNICE. Uh-huh. Uh-huh. I pray my tits look better in this outfit then they do. That's what I would pray for.

SHE bursts out laughing in a delayed beat. CHARLOTTE is genuinely scared.

BERNICE. Well. Don't stand there like a stalker. Come in.

CHARLOTTE sits.

BERNICE. *(Into intercom)* Mary. See that we're not interrupted.

MARY (OFF-STAGE). Yes, Ms. Snell.

BERNICE. Damn. You just interrupted me! By saying that -- you just. Never mind!

MARY (OFF-STAGE). Yes, Ms. Snell.

BERNICE rolls her eyes.

CHARLOTTE. Charlotte Burdick, my pleasure.

She reaches out to shake BERNICE's hand.

BERNICE. I don't shake. A little germaphobic. I use anti-bacterial gel. *(Into intercom)*
Mary? *(Nothing)* Mary? *(Nothing)* Oh crap. Mary -- you can interrupt you lazy bitch!

MARY (OFF-STAGE). *(HER usual droll)* Yes, Ms. Snell.

BERNICE. Where's my anti-bacterial gel?

MARY (OFF-STAGE). Do you want me to run into the supply closet and get another quart?

BERNICE. Forget it. Later you'll lather up and give me a full body scrub.

MARY (OFF-STAGE). Goodie. I'll skip lunch, Ms. Snell.

BERNICE. *(To Charlotte)* Have a seat. I've been looking forward to seeing your work.

CHARLOTTE. You have? You don't know what that means to me...

BERNICE. I say that to everybody without meaning it, don't get your smile going and all.

CHARLOTTE. I want to thank you so much for this opportunity.

BERNICE. I don't have to tell you St. Fabiola is going to be one of the great churches built in the twenty-first century in America.

CHARLOTTE. I hear only good things.

BERNICE. Of course. I'm in charge.

CHARLOTTE. -- Except for the *dreidel* incident.

BERNICE. *(With an evil glare)* What do you know about the... *dreidel* incident?

CHARLOTTE. Well, I was throwing up in the ladies room...

BERNICE. Minor misunderstanding between executive -- me -- and the suppliers. We're opening on schedule, Ms. Burdick, I can assure you of that.

CHARLOTTE. Absolutely. I didn't want to join Poxner and Poser Architects because they are on schedule anyway, Ms. Snell.

BERNICE. Why did you want to join Poxner and Poser Architects?

CHARLOTTE. I wanted to join Poxner and Poser Architects because of you Ms. Snell. I just never knew you were a --

BERNICE. *(Interrupts)* I suppose everyone wants to work with me.

CHARLOTTE. Unless they're afraid. I have followed your career from the beginning. From Columbia University, to apprenticing at Schmitdt and Young. Your very first design. The Harvey Meat Packing Building in New York.
BERNICE. Oh you liked that one?

CHARLOTTE. I wouldn't get my meat anyplace else. I lived in New York four years just to get my meat there. And I'm a Vegetarian. I'd go and admire the details. And your Donnavan Library in Indianapolis. I'd returned books I never even checked out just to sit there. St. Fabiola... From what I've read, it's going to be your crowning achievement.

BERNICE. If... if I had the perfect mural.

CHARLOTTE. I brought sketches.

BERNICE. I'll be kind as always.

CHARLOTTE opens HER portfolio crashing things off the desk.

BERNICE. Don't be nervous. You're only human. Let me see... Yes... *(Holds up one drawing)* Uh-huh uh-huh. Interesting. I see you went with a religious theme.

CHARLOTTE. It's a church, *Sister.*

BERNICE. Sister? That's cute. You call me Bernice. Hmm. I see you have here on this side... the hand of god.

CHARLOTTE. Reaching out...

BERNICE. Reaching out to...

CHARLOTTE. That's The Man. Representing all mankind.

BERNICE. Very original. And... what's this in the corner?

CHARLOTTE. That's the Devil.

BERNICE. I see. And the devil in the picture represents...

CHARLOTTE. The Devil.

BERNICE. Uh-huh. Uh-huh. In the church, they might not want to go this way. I'm not sure, but I can see your train of thought.

CHARLOTTE. Thank you.

BERNICE. Let's look at the others, shall we? *(Picks up another one)* Jesus in the Manger.

CHARLOTTE. That's one of my favorite ones.

BERNICE. And he's a little baby but he has his fist raised up.

CHARLOTTE. He's yelling at God.

BERNICE. That's a middle finger.

CHARLOTTE. He's really *peeved.*

BERNICE. Yelling at god with a middle finger -- Little Jesus pissed off at something, is he?

CHARLOTTE. Upset about the inhumanity here on earth.

BERNICE. Voicing his opinion at such a young age -- reminds me of <u>me</u>. Well it certainly is throwing the church a curve.

CHARLOTTE. He's perturbed about the evils. The hurricanes. The tsunamis. And... very upset about the voting on "American Idol."

BERNICE. Well that would piss off a young baby Jesus, true.

MARY (OFF-STAGE). Ms. Snell, may I interrupt a moment?

BERNICE. *(Into intercom)* Damn you, Mary. Do not interrupt me under any circumstances.

MARY (OFF-STAGE). Word from the construction site, Ms. Snell. Father Johnson is very upset about the location of the confessionary. They're next to the men's room.

BERNICE. Well why didn't you interrupt me, you cow? (SHE looks over the plans) Christ. Well it's all purging, right? Tell the father to keep his collar on, and I'll see what I can do.

MARY (OFF-STAGE). He's crying, Ms. Snell.

BERNICE. Crying? Who is he the Pope? Okay, tell him to hold off on the *stigmata* and wait for me to get there! And I'm not to be interrupted again, Mary!

MARY (OFF-STAGE). Yes, Ms. Snell.

BERNICE. She did it again. She interrupted me.

CHARLOTTE. You're a little brash for a religious person.

BERNICE. Religion. That's a crock.

CHARLOTTE. But you're... you're a...

BERNICE. Look what they got me wearing. Stupid thing. You can't see my hips! Or my sexy ass. And I have a fantastic ass. *(SHE shows CHARLOTTE who turns away)* Not an ass girl?

CHARLOTTE. I feel very uncomfortable hearing about sexy asses and while you are in your sacrament, Ms. Snell.

BERNICE. My what? I feel like a giant mallomar in here. And you can't see my cleavage which is a damn shame. Sometimes I hate this job.

CHARLOTTE. Being a nun?

BERNICE. Being an architect. I'm not a nun.

CHARLOTTE. You're --

BERNICE. Oh you moronic undergrad. This was for a fund-raiser. You thought I was a <u>real</u> nun?

CHARLOTTE. Thank goodness.

BERNICE. I know nothing about being a nun, lady. Or about building a church for that matter. But I'm playing the game. Like you, I have risen to the charge. Brought my entire soul to the cause. *(SHE looks at another drawing)* You've drawn the cross.

CHARLOTTE. Yes. Jesus was put on the cross. Did you know that?

BERNICE. In fact however, your cross has someone else hanging from it.

CHARLOTTE. Regis Philbin.

BERNICE. That would be Regis Philbin.

CHARLOTTE. -- Mr. Philbin represents our addiction to television. Our turning our backs on family and moral discussion in favor of reruns and faux-reality programming.

BERNICE. And you think The Bishop would like this in St. Fabiola?

CHARLOTTE. If he has any balls.

CHARLOTTE laughs... exactly as BERNICE did earlier. BERNICE sits.

BERNICE. Is there anything else you want to tell me about yourself, Miss Burdick?

CHARLOTTE. <u>I'm an atheist</u>!

BERNICE. *(Sarcastic)* I'm shocked.

CHARLOTTE. In fact... Not only am I sure there is no god, but I can prove it. Here you are dressed like a nun.

BERNICE. For a fund-raiser.

CHARLOTTE. -- If there was an almighty, he would be very angry at you. It's blasphemy. Maybe strike you down for insulting nuns everywhere.

BERNICE. You think?

CHARLOTTE. Your use of bad language... and using his name in vein. But he doesn't do anything.

BERNICE. I feel fine.

CHARLOTTE. He lets it slide.

BERNICE. Never felt better in my life. And I didn't even take my tricyclic antidepressant today.

CHARLOTTE. Doesn't even comment on it by making it rain hard or thunder clap.

BERNICE. *(Into intercom)* Mary? Is the sky blue today?

MARY (OFF-STAGE). Clear skies, Ms. Snell. *(BERNICE is about to speak)* Winds south at 10 miles per hour. *(BERNICE is about to speak)* Humidity 59%. *(BERNICE is about to speak)* Dew point. 53 degrees. *(BERNICE is about to speak)* UV Index. Two.

BERNICE. Shut up, Mary.

MARY (OFF-STAGE). Yes, Ms. Snell.
CHARLOTTE. Watch this. *(Looks up)* I HATE YOU! *(At HER)* Nothing.

BERNICE. He's ignoring you completely

CHARLOTTE. I draw pictures of his greatest patrons. His son even. I mock him with my drawings. But he takes no revenge upon me. I'm still alive. Healthy. I never go to confession. And I've wished bad things on many other people.

BERNICE. You seem so innocent.

CHARLOTTE. I hoped the other artist coming in for this very assignment would be hit by a truck, or get a social disease so horrible that I would get the job.

BERNICE. I coveted my neighbor. And my neighbor's neighbor -- when my neighbor wasn't home.

CHARLOTTE. I lie. I've cheated. I have not totally honored thy father or thy mother.

BERNICE. I have in times, purposely dishonored both those freaks.

CHARLOTTE. And I don't keep the Sabbath.

BERNICE. We are actually taunting God.

CHARLOTTE. If there *was* a god.

BERNICE. -- And if there was a god, he would bring his wrath down upon us and teach us a good lesson.

CHARLOTTE. So there can't be. What's the purpose of having an all powerful one, if he never punishes?

BERNICE. Hey. I got another one. I got another test.

SHE leans in and kisses CHARLOTTE on the mouth.

CHARLOTTE. OH my God -- what kind of test was that?

BERNICE. HOMOSEXUALITY, BABY!

CHARLOTTE. I can't believe you just did that during a job interview. And dressed like a nun.

BERNICE. Oh I can fix that.

SHE starts to take her top off.

CHARLOTTE. No!

BERNICE. It's Sexual harassment. God has got to do something now.

THEY both look up, but all is silent.

BERNICE. You know I always thought... hey, there has to be a god, I mean, why else would everyone be so busy talking about him if he didn't exist? Now I'm thinking... if I haven't been struck down -- the way I talk to people, the way I run my business, even how I've treated you here today... then it's a clear case for the absolute definitive conclusion that there is no higher power. Get your lips over here... I'm kissing you again.

BERNICE chases CHARLOTTE.

CHARLOTTE. I've never kissed a girl.

BERNICE. Me either. But I bet you if God *was* up there... He wouldn't make anything taste so good be so wrong.

CHARLOTTE. Stop!

THEY both freeze.

BERNICE. What? You wanna screw? That'll really pissed Him off.

CHARLOTTE. He's not going to be pissed off.

BERNICE. Then you believe He's up there?

CHARLOTTE. Look. If... if he is watching us... he wouldn't get angry because he made us this way. He made you a cantankerous hard nose difficult to-deal-with, impossible job interviewer. And he gave me extraordinary talent for an art school dropout.

BERNICE. *(SHE sits)* People <u>are</u> afraid of me. Afraid to speak up and get fired. Maybe I <u>am</u> a cold, hard person. Maybe I should soften. Charlotte. All those things we taunted God with... all those reasons he should punish us... what if... what if he brought you here to me today in order for me to <u>recognize</u> him? To know that the way I've been behaving is punishable. But instead of hurting me, striking me dead with a bolt of powerful lightening, he's letting me change. And grow. And love him. All by myself.

CHARLOTTE. No. He brought me here to get a job. I need work.

BERNICE. He's teaching me to be more human. To love his words.

CHARLOTTE. No. It's for my health insurance.

BERNICE. I've seen the light.

CHARLOTTE. I've seen a dentist and I need a root canal I can't afford.

BERNICE. *(Covering up)* Please forgive me, My Savior for my inappropriate lack of dress code. His mighty hand could crush me -- but instead, his mighty brain has given me free will.

CHARLOTTE. Are you sending me directly to human resources, because I can start today.

BERNICE. You've given me the Lord's word, Charlotte. It wouldn't be right if I hired you for such a menial task. *(Glances at the drawings)* And with sketches like those. No... You've proven God is watching me. Religion is in my life now. In my blood, and permeating my entire office. No more sleeping around. No more cursing or treating my secretary Mary like dirt.

MARY (OFF-STAGE). Thank you, Miss Snell.

BERNICE. *(Runs to the intercom)* Shut your face, Mary, I'm being healed by the Lord.

MARY (OFF-STAGE). Yes, Ms. Snell.

BERNICE. *(To CHARLOTTE)* I realize now divorcing five men <u>was</u> inappropriate.

CHARLOTTE. No surprise St. Fabiola is the Patron Saint of Divorced People.

BERNICE. I've been a loser and a whore.

CHARLOTTE. No.

BERNICE. Yes. Ask anyone.

MARY (OFF-STAGE). She's been a loser and a whore.

BERNICE. See. And I <u>pay</u> her. *(Ushers CHARLOTTE to the door)* Charlotte Burdick... Go. Go out and spread your consecrated word. And maybe someday we can work on a project together where you don't insult the Big Guy Upstairs.

CHARLOTTE. Are you sure? I really need this job--

BERNICE. Uh-huh. Uh-huh.

And SHE practically pushes CHARLOTTE out. Then moves to the intercom.

BERNICE. Mary?

MARY (OFF-STAGE). Yes, Ms. Snell?

BERNICE. I'm heading back over to the fund-raiser. *(Fixing the habit)* I must speak with Father Johnson. Fix the *dreidel* incident. I want to be nice, Mary. God won't let me be happy until I prove I am worth saving. I'm going to be kind and considerate. Loyal and supportive. And then someone can love me. And I can finally get off Simethicone -- for my infuriating flatulence. Yes, Mary... I'm going to join the church!

BERNICE exits.

MARY (OFF-STAGE). Yes, Ms. Snell? Ms. Snell? Joseph and *Haysuse* are back from the site. Are you there? She's out of the office, boys. Yeah. Another revelation. Today she wanted to be gay. Every week something else. She'll never change. She can't. Why do you think they threw her out of the nunnery?

SHE laughs exactly like BERNICE and CHARLOTTE did earlier.

LIGHTS SLOWLY FADE TO BLACK.

THE MODERN AMERICAN ROMANCE NOT OFTEN SEEN

A small SoHo apartment with an open kitchen. A ratty sofa, center, and a straight back chair that faces it, is the only furniture. The front door is kicked opened and DEEDEE FISHMAN enters, dragging a paralyzed AVERY MINOWITZ from under his shoulders. HIS head can move and look around, but HIS body is limp. SHE drags...

DEEDEE. *(Calmly)* I really had a great time... I'm so glad you came back to see my place. And wasn't that the scariest movie? The uncle -- who would have guessed it was the uncle living in the attic? I want to thank you. I want to thank you for a great date, and please thank your mom for setting us up. I really had a great time, Avery.

AVERY. *(Just as calm)* I can't feel my toes.

DEEDEE. *(Pulls HIM to the sofa; placidly)* I thought the chicken was very good. Did you like your pasta primavera? I'd never tasted such a great sauce... really good stuff. And thanks again for the wine. I usually don't drink with a new boyfriend, but we were laughing so much, I figured why not? I think it's so funny that your brother and my sister went to Francis Lewis High School together. Small world, small world.

AVERY. *(Tries to lift a hand, cannot)* I seem to be slightly... immobile.

DEEDEE. I love that shirt on you. That color... you have to remind me around your birthday, I want to buy you more shirts that color. Would that be alright with you?

AVERY. I can blink. That I can do. *(Blinks)* Blink.

DEEDEE. Oh I forgot... I bought you something.

SHE leans AVERY'S head up on the side of the sofa and exits. Unable to stay upright, HE flops over. SHE enters with a large lollipop.

DEEDEE. Remember? Remember we passed that candy place on Bleeker and you said this looked delicious? *(HE nods; SHE sits HIM up)* I bought it for you. I bought it for you, Avery. Do you know why I bought it for you? *(HE shakes HIS head)* Because we passed that candy place on Bleeker and you said this looked delicious. *(SHE slides in next to HIM)* And because I like you. *(SHE unwraps the lollipop and allows HIM to lick it)* Good?

AVERY. My legs are tingling.

DEEDEE. It's nothing. Listen, Avery, I got tickets to "Mamma Mia" for Saturday. I'd really like to go with you.

AVERY. *(Stares at HIS hand)* My fingers aren't moving.

DEEDEE. It's nothing. They're great seats. Oo -- let me show you what I'm going to wear.

SHE exits. AVERY tries to move but winds up face first on the floor. DEEDEE enters in a low-cut short dress showing off as much as possible.

DEEDEE. I know, I know... I'm gorgeous! Avery -- what happened? *(SHE sits HIM up then pulls HIM up onto the sofa)* You are so funny. Really witty. Remember our first date... you were telling jokes left and right. And right and left!

AVERY. Deedee?

DEEDEE. Yes, boyfriend?

AVERY. There's any reason why I can't feel my body?

DEEDEE. Yes, future husband.

AVERY. And what is that reason, Deedee?

DEEDEE. I slipped you a *Flunitrazepam.*

AVERY. Did I need a Flunitrazepam?

DEEDEE. Oh yes, future father-to-breed-my-children. You definitely needed a Flunitrazepam.

AVERY. Did it come with the pasta primavera?

DEEDEE. You are sooo funny. Left and right. And right and left.

AVERY. Deedee, what is a Flunitrazepam?

DEEDEE. It's a, future co-life insurance policy partner-holder. Hey, look at the shoes I got to go with this outfit. *(Exits. Returns with 12 inch spiked heels... hooker-style)* At first I thought they were a little on the short side, then I realized you liked my legs, so why not show them off?

AVERY. I like your legs?

DEEDEE. You told me last week. When we met. When you fell for me. The first time we made love.

AVERY. We never...

DEEDEE. -- You boys forget so easily. You think I made this stuff up?

AVERY. Deedee... did you make that stuff up? That we made love last week?

DEEDEE. I exaggerated. Is that a crime now in your John Ashcroft world?

AVERY. *(Running out of patience)* What did you give me?

DEEDEE. *(Sits, pulls shoes off and takes off dress... now in silk flimsy slip. Calmly)* It's an innocent R-2. Or a... street *shay*, mind-eraser drug. It just attacks your central nervous system's all.

AVERY. *(Worried; struggles to move)* I'm paralyzed!

DEEDEE. -- It's your standard depressant that's ten times more powerful than Valium.

AVERY. Because Valium wasn't strong enough to drug me with?

DEEDEE. *(Laughing uncontrollably)* Funny left and right. And right and l...

AVERY. I'm scared, Deedee. I'm really scared. Where did you get --?

DEEDEE. -- The chic I bought it from tells me in some foreign countries it's used as a pre-surgical sedative and for treatment of severe sleep and psychiatric disorders. Doesn't it make you feel like we've traveled abroad together?

AVERY. We can't travel abroad -- I can't move! Why did you do this?
DEEDEE. I just wanted your attention for one night.

AVERY. I have an itch... nose nose nose...

SHE scratches it for HIM.

AVERY. This is horrible. This is horrible. My mother should know this has been a horrible date.

DEEDEE. But we're growing closer.

AVERY. Closer? You gave me the date rape drug?

DEEDEE. If you call it that -- you take all the fun out of it.

AVERY. This is a crime! This is against the law. The last thing I remember we were having a very nice conversation at a quaint chic restaurant on Hauser, and you offered me a drink.

DEEDEE. It wasn't just a nice conversation, Avery. You were going to break up with me.

AVERY. I was not.

DEEDEE. You weren't?

AVERY. No.

DEEDEE. I misread you. I shouldn't have crushed two colorless, odorless, tasteless sedatives into your Petite Syrah.

AVERY. TWO?!

DEEDEE. I thought you were dumping me.

AVERY. It was only our second date.

DEEDEE. Sometimes guys can be very non-committal.

AVERY. I have an itch... ear ear ear.

SHE scratches HIM.

AVERY. I never heard of this happening. We innocently sat down... ordered a meal...

DEEDEE. Boy. That pasta primavera had great sauce.

AVERY. -- And you said, "Let me go get us something from the bar."

DEEDEE. I had to put the drugs into your drink so you wouldn't see me. Aren't you proud? I did it all by myself.

AVERY. Deedee... you've done a terrible thing. A completely immoral unforgiveable disturbing thing.

DEEDEE. You want another suck of the lolly?

AVERY. I want you jailed!

DEEDEE. Men never see it from our point of view.
AVERY. Well I guess I do now -- because my eyes are the only thing working!

DEEDEE. Do you know what's out there? The horrors? Oh no. When we get a guy who... who shows us a little caring. A little friendship. Or even... a little love... well... we hold on to it. We grab on to it and choke it tight.

AVERY. NOW you wanna choke me?

DEEDEE. No, no, my dear, Avery. I would never hurt you. *(HE throws HER a look)* Permanently. I just don't want to lose you to someone who can offer you more.

AVERY. I wasn't interested in someone who could offer me more.

DEEDEE. Even to someone with bigger tits.

AVERY. I liked <u>you</u>. I liked your sense of humor and your smile. I liked the feeling of your hand in mine. You have to give these things time to grow.

DEEDEE. *(Looks at HER breasts)* They're fully grown.

AVERY. I'm talking about love! You rushed things.

DEEDEE. I should let it all happen in a natural course... evolve like a true love affair.

AVERY. You pushed it. That's why I'm sitting in my own feces from the pasta primavera.

DEEDEE. I guess I wear my emotions right on my sleeve.

AVERY. Get me my phone... I'm calling my mother. This is the last time I let her set me up with a psychotic.

DEEDEE. *(Reaches for the phone)* You don't have to be rude.

AVERY. *(She takes the phone from his pocket)* Can you open it? Can you please open it? *(She opens it)* Can you press one? Can you please press one? *(SHE dials it)* Can you hold it, can you please hold it? *(SHE holds it to HIS ear. Into phone)* Mom? *(Breaks down)* Mommy... I can't move. *(Stronger)* Yes, mom. I did go out with Deedee Fishman, like you told me. After our first date I had a good time and wanted to see her again.

DEEDEE. *(Screams into phone)* Hello, Mrs. Minowitz.

AVERY. She says hi and wants to know how the pasta primavera was.

DEEDEE. Great sauce.

AVERY. *(Into phone)* Mom. How well did you know Deedee Fishman before you set me up with her? How desperate do you think I am? How lonely can a man be to put himself into a situation like this? *(Long beat)* Huh? We're going to talk about this later, Mother. Goodbye. Can you hang up? Can you please hang up? *(DEEDEE takes the phone)* She wants to know if the ruffie she sold you worked out alright.

DEEDEE. I hope you told her it did.

AVERY. THE WOMAN IS A FREAK!

DEEDEE. I felt you pulling away, Avery.
AVERY. I wasn't pulling -- and now I can't pull anything! *(HE falls over and DEEDEE holds HIM up)*
She said she wanted me to give you a shot. A chance. She said I always break up with girls too soon without...

DEEDEE. -- Without what?

AVERY. Without letting things... evolve. Like a true love affair. Guess I wear *my* emotions right on my sleeve too.

DEEDEE. If I try to kiss you... will you pull away?

AVERY. HOW?

SHE gently kisses HIM.

AVERY. Again?

DEEDEE. Got it.

AVERY. So when does this stuff wear off? *(Beat)* Soon I hope.

DEEDEE. Soon enough for you to put your arms around me the next time we kiss.

AVERY. Wanna make some popcorn and watch a movie?

DEEDEE. The TV's in the bedroom.

AVERY. I don't mind going in the bedroom.

DEEDEE. *(Shyly)* It's our second date, Avery... are you suggesting we make love?

AVERY. Well, we don't want to rush things. We should wait until the drug wears off.

DEEDEE drags a limp AVERY toward the bedroom.

DEEDEE. *(Laughs)* Funny left and right and right and --

As SHE drags HIM...

LIGHTS OUT.

HOOD RATZ

Set: A living room in an apartment in the Fairfax District of Los Angeles. Sofa center, chair and table. Door, upstage, right.

Time: Early Morning.

Lights up: BEN KATZ, 30s, stands center, dressed in corporate button down short sleeve shirt, dark slacks, and leather shoes. HE attempts to put on Tefillin(phylacteries). BEN is not great at it. HE looks more like a mummy with the leather straps hanging loose and awkward. HE grows frustrated but hides it well.

ARTHUR (OFF-STAGE) Ben! You think we're much alike? *(Beat)* You think we're alike? Similar?

ARTHUR, his brother, enters, also awkwardly bound in the Tefillin leather straps hanging loosely off HIS arm and head. HE is dressed identical. HE doesn't hide HIS frustration.

ARTHUR. I feel like I've been attacked by giant licorice.

BEN. Brothers are brothers. Similar is similar. Same beliefs, same problems, same dreams, same same. Ready? *(Prays)* Baruch ata Adonai elohanynu melech ha'olam asher kidshanu bemitzvotav vetzivanu lehani'ach Tefillin. They say when you grow up with someone, you take on the habits of the other person. Nature vs. Nurture. Ready? *(Prays)* Baruch ata Adonai elohanynu melech ha'olam asher kidshanu bemitzvotav vetzivanu al mitzvat Tefillin.

ARTHUR. Hey, Look. It's "Snakes on A Plane."

BEN. We can't forget that the two of us grew up for most of our lives without a mother and father. Think about it, Arthur. If you had grown up with a gorilla, you would take on the habits of such gorilla.

ARTHUR. I don't want to be a gorilla, Ben.

BEN. None of us do. *(Prays) Baruch Shem Kvod Malchuso Leolam Vaed.*

BEN/ARTHUR. *Amen.*

BEN. -- There's nothing to worry about, Arthur. I've taken care of you since momma and poppa went to heaven, and I will continue to take care of you no matter what. Now take off your Tefillin, we'll have some breakfast. I made your favorite.

ARTHUR. Blintzes?

BEN. Toast. Then we'll go to work. I packed a lunch. Your favorite.

ARTHUR. Peanut butter and jelly?

BEN. Roast chicken and mustard.

ARTHUR. *(As HE packs the Tefillin)* I never did get used to putting these things on.

BEN. You see? We're practically twins in this respect. So we do it.

ARTHUR. We do it wrong.

BEN. All the time. But we try. Always trying. And if he, *hashem*, wills it, we will keep trying.
ARTHUR. And soon there will be three of us, right, Ben? Three of us.

BEN. Arthur, if God is on our side, if he, *hashem,* wills it, then we will be a united family. For the first time. Just think of it. After all these years, a brother.

ARTHUR. A new brother.

BEN. Huh? Yes! So when the private detective calls --

ARTHUR. She called, Ben. The private detective.

BEN. She called? Why didn't you tell me she called? Arthur! What did she say?

ARTHUR. She said she's coming right over. To give us news.

BEN. Clean up, Arthur... this could be it. This could be the news we've been praying for.

As THEY tidy up, the doorbell rings.

BEN. Get the door. I'll put out some treats... Your favorite...

ARTHUR. Cotton candy?

BEN. Chocolates. Go, go, go.

BEN puts a box of chocolates on the table as ARTHUR opens the door and SALLY PEABODY enters. SHE wears a black trench coat, and large fedora. SHE is slightly Sam Spade so far as to enter the room and shadow the wall as if being followed. SHE speaks with a thick Russian accent.

ARTHUR. Miss Peabody.

SALLY. Anybody else here?

ARTHUR points to BEN.

BEN. I have a chicken in the kitchen. I was making lunch.

SALLY. When you hired me, I had no idea the journey I was going to undertake. The places I would see, and the people I would meet. I travelled to New York, and London. Spain and Madrid. *(SHE looks around to make sure nobody caught her lie)* I backpacked, and rode motor scooters. Logged frequent flyer miles and learned to pull a rickshaw. And finally I have the most amazing news.

ARTHUR. You found our brother.

SALLY. *(SHE speaks without the accent...it was a fake)* Why'd you ruin it for me? I wanted to be the one to tell you. *(Frustrated)* All right. All right. Through exhaustive means... your parents identification, DNA testing, and cross-checking facts and figures... I have found the boy that your momma and poppa gave up when they were young teenagers.

ARTHUR. I could cry.

BEN. *(About to cry)* Stay strong, Arthur. The Katz men stay strong.

ARTHUR. Tell us more, Miss Peabody. Does he look like us?

SALLY. The resemblance is striking.
BEN. Imagine that. Imagine that, Arthur.

SALLY. *(Russian accent)* -- And you won't in a million years guess where your long lost brother actually lives.

ARTHUR. Right in this neighborhood.

SALLY. Why'd you ruin it for me? I wanted to be the one to tell you.

BEN. Arthur, stop ruining it for her. He lives around here.

ARTHUR. It's like mother and father are back with us.

BEN. It's a miracle. It's the miracle of Passover.

ARTHUR. It is?

BEN. Yes of course. The Jewish people -- exiled from the Land of Goshen after the plagues were brought down upon Egypt. We have been plagued, Arthur. A shroud has always been over us wondering if our older brother was safe. Happy. And if he carried on the traditions of our family.

ARTHUR. *(To SALLY)* Then he wants to meet us.

SALLY. Are you going to <u>continually</u> ruin this for me?

BEN. Arthur. Please. Miss Peabody, have you met him? Have you met our brother yet?

SALLY. I have. We had dinner last night.

BEN. Dinner?

SALLY. Last night. It was very romantic.

BEN. It was, why?

ARTHUR. -- So he eats. *(THEY look at HIM)* Oh I knew my brother would eat. I love him already.

BEN. Might I ask -- Was it a Kosher meal, Miss Peabody?

SALLY. Your brother is Glatt Kosher, Ben. The biggest Kosher anyone can be. And he's a big tipper. And hands, very soft.

BEN. Excuse me...?

ARTHUR. He's Kosher, Ben. Our brother is Kosher. Miss Peabody, what did my brother eat?

SALLY. Blintzes.

BEN. Oh my Lord, Arthur... did you hear that?

ARTHUR. Blintzes are my favorite food. Next to *kishka*, potato *latke*, and Popeyes Fried Chicken.

BEN. *(To HER)* What did he say at dinner, Miss Peabody? What are his intentions?

SALLY. Oh we talked about many things. All night long in fact. He has a beautiful baritone voice.
BEN. What? No, no... Did he speak about his childhood?

ARTHUR. He had a childhood, didn't he?

SALLY. Your brother <u>had</u> a childhood, Arthur.

ARTHUR. So he was a child! I knew it! I knew my brother would have been a child.

SALLY. He spoke kindly of his adoptive parents.

BEN. And they were of the Jewish persuasion?

SALLY. Freakin' big Jews.

ARTHUR. He's a Jew!

BEN. *(Arms raised high)* YES!

ARTHUR and BEN dance around the sofa like an impromptu "<u>Hava Nagila.</u>*"*

BEN. Miss Peabody. May I ask? Did he attend Yeshiva?

SALLY. He did, Ben. As a young man.

BEN. Arthur! Our brother was a Yeshiva student.

ARTHUR. A Yeshiva student who was a child and who eats. Holy Cow!

One more dance around the sofa.

BEN. It's another miracle. The miracle of Hanukkah.

ARTHUR. It is?

BEN. Yes of course. The Jewish people only had enough oil to make the menorah light for one night. But it lasted eight nights. We thought it was just the two of us, Arthur. Two boys without parents left alone to fend for themselves. It turns out there is enough love for three. Three! *(To SALLY)* So you had dinner, then...

SALLY. Well obviously we went dancing -- duh.

ARTHUR and BEN look at each other.

SALLY. Then this morning at his apartment...

BEN. You were at his apartment this morning?

ARTHUR. Our brother's apartment?

BEN. You spent the night?

SALLY. We had a very nice breakfast together. French toast.

ARTHUR. Oh I hope he's not French, Ben.
BEN. Miss Peabody, are you telling us you had breakfast, after having dinner and spending the night with him? What is going on, Miss Peabody?

SALLY. I have been insulted, Mr. Katz. I am a professional often horny private investigator. Licensed by this state under a grant to an off-shore internet site that I paid twelve dollars to. I was doing my job. Slowly getting to know this man. Man to woman. Woman to man. Hot hot woman to man. And I have come to the conclusion that he is the perfect husband -- <u>brother</u>. I said brother!

BEN. Miss Peabody -- you are dating our long lost brother!

SALLY. -- I'm going to be paid, right? Paid?

ARTHUR. What's his name?

SALLY. His name?

BEN. Did you get his name while you were eating and dancing and waking up in his apartment for French toast this morning?

SALLY. His name is Yewande.

ARTHUR. His name is Yewande?

BEN. Yehuda?

SALLY. Yewande.

BEN. Yehuda?

SALLY. His name is Yewande.

ARTHUR. It's an interesting name. Do you think momma named him that, Ben?

BEN. Is it from the Old Testament?

ARTHUR. It sounds old.

SALLY. *(Russian accent)* I have one more surprise.

ARTHUR. He's coming here right now.

SALLY. Okay, you're not making this fun for me at all.

The doorbell rings.

SALLY. It's your brother.

BEN. Why am I so nervous all of a sudden? The Katz men never get nervous.

ARTHUR. I should put out something to eat. Cuz he eats! *(HE puts out chocolates)* Chocolate!

BEN. Our brother. Our Jewish brother. Open the door, Arthur. Go, go, go.

ARTHUR opens the door, and a tall, muscular, bald, African American man in "wife beater" top and very tight jeans, enters, smiling broadly.

YEWANDE. My *Mishpucha!*

BEN. Holy shit.

ARTHUR. Hide the silverware!

YEWANDE. It's a *hekaya.*

BEN. <u>And</u> he's an illegal alien who doesn't speak English.

SALLY. Everyone. I would like you to meet your brother. The very handsome, broad-shouldered, sexier than all hell -- Yewande.

ARTHUR. His name is Yewande.

BEN. Yehuda?

SALLY. Yewande.

BEN. Yehuda?

SALLY. This is Arthur and Ben Katz. Your brothers.

YEWANDE. Yewande Manatoba.

BEN. Manatoba? That is definitely <u>not</u> from the Old Testament.

ARTHUR. Are you part of the Manatoba family that put in the swimming pool at Torah Et Sh'ma Temple on Pico?

YEWANDE. No. I'm part of the Manatoba family that came from Angola in the underbelly of a slave ship and built up most of Savannah.

ARTHUR. *(To BEN)* I'm sure they're very nice people too.

SALLY. Why don't you sit down, Yewande?

BEN. Yehuda?

SALLY/ARTHUR. <u>Yewande!</u>

BEN throws THEM a look.

SALLY. Next to me would be fine.

SHE yanks YEWANDE so hard HE goes flying to sit next to HER.

YEWANDE. *Ahsante. (To the others)* It means "Thank You."

There is cold silence until ARTHUR leans in to BEN.

ARTHUR. Say something, Ben, he's scaring me.

BEN. So Sally tells us your name is --

YEWANDE. -- Yewande. It's an African Yoruba name. It means "Mother has returned."

ARTHUR. If she did, she'd drop dead of a heart attack.

BEN. Arthur! *(Beat)* Will you excuse me a moment, please, Yehuda.

YEWANDE. Yewande.

BEN. Arthur!

THEY move to stage left, and whisper.

BEN. Hide your wallet. He's clearly after our money and our property.

ARTHUR. We don't have any money or property.

BEN. Then he's after our poverty and our depression.

ARTHUR. Could he really be our long lost brother, Ben?

BEN. You see any similarities? Does he talk like momma?

YEWANDE. Yo, *dog,* you got a nice *crib* here -- really flav... thanks for *representing.* I could certainly *hit skins* with some *boom boom* around here if I was a *gangsta,* but I ain't into meeting some *Jakes.*

ARTHUR. That don't sound like Momma.

SALLY joins THEM.

SALLY. He's smokin' hot, isn't he? I mean I'm not the only one that sees it, right?

BEN. *(To HER)* The resemblance is striking! What's wrong with you? I did not hire you for this to turn into a J-Date, Miss Peabody... That man is not our brother!

SALLY. Why? Because he doesn't look like you, or talk like you? I resent the fact that you think this whole thing was set up just so that you two would pay me and that all I really wanted was to meet a Black Rock God. Like Seal.

BEN. In order for him to be my brother, Miss Peabody, my mother would have had to... have... my mother would have been involved with a... a Katz woman would never...

ARTHUR offers chocolates to YEWANDE.

YEWANDE. *Chakleti! Hawa ya moyo chakleti.(Smiles)* That means I have a deep love for chocolate.

ARTHUR. Me too. You should try the dark ones. Once you've had those, you never go back.

SALLY. Look at the three of you. Like a mirror. *(To BEN)* I'm going to be paid, right? Paid? *(Over to YEWANDE)* Dancing again, tonight, right? Salsa? Merengue? Lap?

BEN. Okay... this is not right. We're Jewish. We have been Jewish for a very long time. Like always! We are <u>very</u> Jewish.

YEWANDE. I betcha my people have been Jewish a lot longer than your people have.

BEN. *(To SALLY)* I want proof. You hear me? I want proof that this man is my brother or you don't get a penny from us.

YEWANDE. -- You want proof?

SALLY. Notice how his muscles tense perfectly when he gets angry. Yumm.

YEWANDE. -- Did you want proof <u>before</u> you met me?

BEN. Yes, Mr. Manatoba. I want proof. Tell them Arthur. If I say I want proof then I want proof.

ARTHUR. Ben wants proof. *(To YEWANDE)* So if you have to beat the crap out of somebody -- it should be *him*.

SALLY. I've done my research, Mr. Katz. It seems that right before your parents were married, your mother had a small, insignificant, affair.

ARTHUR. I don't think he's insignificant, Ben, he's at least a hundred and forty pounds.

BEN. Shut up, Arthur! Go on, Miss Peabody.

SALLY. It was a one night affair. Your father knew about it and helped your mother through the process of birth and then adoption. But they stayed together, and eventually married.

BEN. But how, why... one night? What was so great about this man? This man that almost ruined my life -- who almost kept me from having life -- that now brings this stranger into my world. What was so important about that man?

SALLY. I hear a lot of people are drawn into relationships with their rabbi.

ARTHUR. Momma *shtuped* the rabbi?

YEWANDE. It's a *hekaya*.

BEN. Again with that?! Look I am not buying any of this. A Black rabbi? What is this, San Francisco?

YEWANDE. I'm a rabbi's son. I told you there were lots of us.

BEN. I have to sit down. *(Sits. Stares at YAWENDE)* I have nothing in common with you.

YEWANDE. We have the Torah.

BEN. Totally overrated.

ARTHUR. Ben!

BEN. I don't know what I'm saying.

YEWANDE. We have the Five Books of Moses. We have the Midrash. We have the thirteen textual tools attributed to the Tanna Rabbi Ishmael used in the interpretation of Jewish Law *halakha*. Of course we have Rabbi Eliezer's narrative of the more important events of the Pentateuch. And we have the popular and oft mentioned religious celebration of *Shmini Atzeres*.

BEN. Do we have a Tylenol?

YEWANDE. So... What do you boys do for a living?

BEN. We're accountants. What do you do?

YEWANDE. I'm a Certified Public Accountant for the state of California in the legislative branch.

ARTHUR. Wow. *(To BEN)* Is that good?

BEN. I'm talking, Arthur! *(To YEWANDE)* Funny how we all became accountants. Eh, Miss Peabody.

YEWANDE. Tell me more about momma.

BEN. *(Forced into it)* Momma was a saint. She raised us to be good thinking scholarly men. To ask the right questions when making decisions. To speak with the rabbi. To honor our people, and our traditions.

ARTHUR. She did more than speak with the rabbi.

ARTHUR. I'm just saying.

YEWANDE. Oh I love the traditions.

SALLY. Isn't he just the dreamiest when he talks *shul?(THEY all look at HER)* Well he is!

YEWANDE. You know what my favorite is? That if you are born to a Jewish mother... you are automatically Jewish. It's a free pass. True. No other religion in the world can say that. There is no birthright for Roman Catholics. You need to be baptized. Muslims. Buddhist. You have to study, you have to work at it. Prove yourself. All we have to do is be born. Oh no... I am as much a Jew as the two of you -- believe me, I know that.

BEN. *(With an unpleasant taste)* Yes. We know that too.

YEWANDE. You don't like the fact that I might be your brother, do you, Ben? *(Rises)* Maybe I can put your minds at ease.

SALLY. Yes, yes he can do that. And after, you and I can skinny dip in the jacuzzi. *(To ARTHUR and Ben)* You do have a jacuzzi, don't you?

BEN. And how are you going to do that, Mr. Manatoba? Put our minds at ease. Tell me how you done good by yourself? Pulled yourself up by your bootstraps? Thought every day and night about what your real mother was like? Eh? Worked your way out of the projects?

SALLY. Yewande grew up in Tarzana.

BEN. Shut! Up!

ARTHUR. *(Whispers to BEN)* Do they have projects in Tarzana, Ben?

BEN. Would you please stay out of this, Arthur? *(To Yewande)* Make your case. Manatoba. Make it and leave.

YEWANDE. I would have done anything to meet my birth mother. You know why? Because... then I would know why I have this feeling... this feeling deep inside of me, gnawing at my bones... biting at my fingertips. To answer that one question. That one undeniable question that has been with me my entire life! *(Beat)* Why is it I love *matzah?*

SALLY. He's so cute with the Hebrew.

BEN. Well, it was really unpleasant meeting you...

ARTHUR. But, Ben...

BEN. Arthur. The Katz men are not like this person. *(To YEWANDE)* I am sure, sometime in the future, you are more than welcome to send us a *Rosh Hashana* card... Get the door, Arthur, go, go, go!

ARTHUR doesn't move.

SALLY. Mr. Katz... You can't just throw him out...

BEN. If you want payment for this, Miss Peabody, see my lawyer.

ARTHUR. *(Finally standing up to HIS brother)* We can't afford a lawyer, Ben.

BEN backs down for the first time.

SALLY. Keep your money. I was just trying to do the right thing. And make a home. A family. Live in Tujunga and raise a shit-load of Manatoba children.

YEWANDE starts to go then stops. ARTHUR moves to shake HIS hand and then YEWANDE does a rapper-style shake which confuses ARTHUR to no end. Then THEY hug.

YEWANDE. Someday, Ben, someday you are going to think of me. That your mother gave me life. And you are going to want to talk to me. Maybe about your family. Or the Torah. Or maybe just to say Shalom. I hope you will.

YEWANDE heads for the door when HE sees the Tefillin on the table. HE laughs.

YEWANDE. Hmm. My dad always laughed when I put these on.

HE starts to go.

ARTHUR. You put on the *Teffillin?* Ben?

THEY watch as YEWANDE puts on the Tefillin <u>perfectly</u>. No strings hanging. He looks great in it.

YEWANDE. *Baruch ata Adonai elohanynu melech ha'olam asher kidshanu bemitzvotav vetzivanu...*

ARTHUR. *(Tries to say it)...* vets... vento... vanooo...

YEWANDE. *(Helps HIM to pronounce)...lehani'ach...*

YEWANDE/ARTHUR. *...lehani'ach... Tefillin.*

ARTHUR. He did it right! Ben! Yewande Manatoba put on the Tefillin correctly. <u>You</u> can't even do that!

BEN. Yeah well... but...

ARTHUR. Similar is <u>not</u> similar.

BEN. Arthur?

ARTHUR. It's the miracle of... of... a... Martin Luther King Day! Momma and Poppa sent Yewande here to teach us. There was no point in them sending another one of <u>us</u>... we need to learn from <u>him</u>. To be good practicing Jews together. To accept all peoples into our lives regardless of creed, or color....

SALLY. *(Re: YEWANDE)* -- Or drop dead gorgeous. I really wish you'd all see the truth in that.

BEN. Poppa always said that one day after he was long gone someone would come into my life and I would know it was meant to be. I was hoping he was talking about Jessica Alba. But no. It's you. You <u>are</u> my brother.

YEWANDE. Well. If he, *hashem,* wills it, it will be.

THEY hug. BEN finally smiles.

SALLY. There's going to be a wedding! *(THEY all look at HER)* Okay, I'm going to be pai--?

BEN. *(Interrupts)* -- You <u>will</u> be paid, Miss Peabody. For bringing us... a Katz Man. Come. I'm taking everybody out for a meal.

ARTHUR/YEWANDE/SALLY. *Blintzes?*

BEN. Word up.

As THEY all start to go...

BEN. Oh. There is one thing I don't get, Miss Peabody. After searching New York, London, Spain and... Madrid... and riding a motor scooter, how <u>did</u> you find our brother right here?

SALLY. Well the truth is I was visiting this temple in Encino and there's a bar next door. In walks Yewande. We hit it off. He tells me his life story and I put two and two together. I just got lucky.

BEN. I didn't think you went to Madrid.

ARTHUR. Maybe it's a *hekaya*.

BEN. WHAT THE HELL DOES THAT MEAN?

YEWANDE. It means -- miracle.

THEY all nod as THEY exit. BLACKOUT.

<u>*END OF SHOW.*</u>

Other Plays by Mark Troy

The Bitter Herbs
(3m 3f.)
A collection of five short plays that depict American Jewish life for the Passover season that make up one evening of theater. "Mark Troy has an easy way with words... This diverting work concerns heightened situations that any might encounter. The whole evening is a giggle, well-rendered...if it won't make you think, it will make you laugh...and you don't have to be Jewish." Backstage West.

The Secret Nymph of New Hyde Park
(6m 3f.)
A New York Senator finds out his wife has some extra political activities in order to raise money for his run. "'The Secret Nymph' is a wild and woolly romp... go along with a gag, a giggle or a guffaw (in this) zany sex farce and savvy political satire whipped together into a froth of frenzied absurdity." Drama-Logue

Tsuris
(4m 5f.)
Retirement in Century Village never looked so facocked when two lovers meet only to find out their aging parents are having an affair. "Comic tribulations aplenty...over-the-top orgy of Borscht-Belt-flavored slap-stick." IN-Magazine Los Angeles

Paging Dr. Chutzpah
(2m 3f.)
Psychiatrist Lester Oronofsky is New York's most disreputable doctor... and now he has to train his own nephew in his footsteps. "A saucy boulevard romp. A lewd and lunatic study that kicks the Catskills style into a place somewhere between Woody Allen and Hooters. Troy has a talent for outsized patter, and he certainly layers on the situational dynamics." Los Angeles Times

Belladonnas of the Court
(3m 3f.)
When a local L.A. neighborhood is scheduled for demolition, the inhabitants must band together to save what little community pride they have. "Mark M Troy's modernistic reflections on gentrification in LA's Fairfax District commands respect with Ionesco style banter.... It's refreshing." LA Weekly

Desperation
(1m 3f.)
Debbie Zlotnik has no idea what she is getting herself into when she is coupled with Gerald Febermiltz after joining the Insta-Mating Dating Service. It's only a matter of time before she finds out that Gerald has murdered the previous two women the dating service has sent over. "'Desperation' displays a remarkable adroit use of language and characterization in the ingenious exploration of male/female relationships." Village View

About the Author

Mark Troy is the winner of the Drury International Playwriting Award Prize for *Mr. Wexler* and The Claire Donaldson Prize for Playwriting for the play *Afterpiece*. Produced, New York: *Desperation* (Samuel French Best Short Play), *The Plot* (Riant Festival Winner), *Jewel Avenue* (Writer's Theater), *A Jewish Booty Call* (Theatre-Studio). Los Angeles; *Tsuris, Paging Dr. Chutzpah* (Sidewalk Studio), *Belladonna's of the Court* (Theatre League, Best Comedy Nom., Brooklyn Publishers), *The Secret Nymph of New Hyde Park* (Renegade Theater), *Peking Duck* (Next Stage), *Homewrecker* (Rose Theatre), *Getting You Bupkus, Misguided Production, Shiksa, Join The Club* (Malibu Stage Winners), *Everyone I Know* (L.A. Play Festival Winner). Others; *Century Village Boca, The Proposal, Birdy* (Actors Theatre of Louisville), Balloon (Chicago Dramatist Winner), *Sister Snell* (Acme, Boston), *How To Marry Your Stalker* (Harrogate, England), *Man on the Mountain* (British Columbia). Mark has had over 50 plays produced around the world. *The Plot* is published (Smith & Kraus) Best Plays of 2007, and *Sister Snell*, Best Plays 2008. His collection of short plays under the title *The Bitter Herbs* is published by Tinsel Road Books. Troy is working on his first musical *Who Gets The House* with composer Lenny Solomon and wrote the original screenplay for *Tooth Fairy* and an early draft of *The Guru*. He also co-wrote *Driving Me Crazy* starring Joe Bologna, Mickey Rooney and Celeste Holm and the horror cult classic *Zipperface*. Troy teaches screenwriting and speaks at many writers conferences. He is a member of the WGA and The Dramatist Guild of America. Please visit Mark Troy on the web at www.curtainrise.com.